Next Time You See a FIREFLY

BY EMILY MORGAN

nsta kids
National Science Teaching Association

Arlington, Virginia

nsta kids
National Science Teaching Association

Claire Reinburg, Director
Jennifer Horak, Managing Editor
Andrew Cooke, Senior Editor
Amanda O'Brien, Associate Editor
Wendy Rubin, Associate Editor
Amy America, Book Acquisitions Coordinator

ART AND DESIGN
Will Thomas Jr., Director

PRINTING AND PRODUCTION
Catherine Lorrain, Director

NATIONAL SCIENCE TEACHERS ASSOCIATION
David L. Evans, Executive Director
David Beacom, Publisher

1840 Wilson Blvd., Arlington, VA 22201
www.nsta.org/store
For customer service inquiries, please call 800-277-5300.

Lexile® measure: 890L

Special thanks to Don Salvatore, firefly watch coordinator at the Boston Museum of Science, and Dr. Keith Summerville, associate professor of environmental science and associate dean at the College of Arts and Sciences at Drake University, for reviewing this manuscript.

Library of Congress Cataloging-in-Publication Data
Morgan, Emily R. (Emily Rachel), 1973-
  Next time you see a firefly / by Emily Morgan. -- 1st ed.
      p. cm.
  "NSTA Kids."
  ISBN 978-1-936959-18-1 (print) -- ISBN 978-1-938946-79-0 (e-book) 1. Fireflies--Juvenile literature. I. National Science Teachers Association. II. Title.
  QL596.L28M67 2013
  595.76'44--dc23
                              2013017767

Cataloging-in-Publication Data are also available from the Library of Congress for the e-book.
LCCN 2013020276

Library binding ISBN: 978-1-938946-16-5

To Jeff, my perfect mate.

"*Every mystery solved brings us to the threshold of a greater one.*"

—Rachel Carson

A NOTE TO PARENTS AND TEACHERS

The books in this series are intended to be read with a child *after* he has had some experience with the featured objects or phenomena. For example, go outside together on a summer evening and watch the fireflies. Notice that some fly around while others perch in the grass or on a bush. Count the seconds between each flash and see if you can detect any patterns in the flashes. Share stories about a time when you caught fireflies as a kid, then gently catch some fireflies and place them in a jar or bug box so you can take a closer look. (Be sure the container allows air in and place a moist piece of paper towel in the bottom so the fireflies won't dry out.) Ask your child what he is wondering about the fireflies, and share what you wonder. Then read this book together and discuss new learnings. You will find that new learnings often lead to new questions. Take time to pause and share these wonderings with each other. Don't forget to let the fireflies go before the night is over. As you'll find out from this book, they have a lot to do!

This book does not present facts to be memorized. It was written to inspire a sense of wonder about these interesting insects and to foster a desire to learn more about the natural world. Children are naturally fascinated by fireflies, and when they learn why fireflies flash and about each species' own flashing pattern, these summertime insects become so much more remarkable. My wish is that after reading this book, you and your child feel a sense of wonder the next time you see a firefly.

—Emily Morgan

Next time you see a firefly, follow it with your eyes. Count the flashes. Do you notice a pattern or rhythm to the flashing? Is the firefly flying, or is it perched on a blade of grass or in a bush? Gently catch a firefly in a net or in your hand. Can you count its legs? Can you see its eyes? Can you find the part of its body that lights up?

Fireflies are one of the most fascinating insects because of their ability to produce light inside their bodies. Have you ever wondered why fireflies flash?

Mating! That's the main reason why fireflies flash. The fireflies you see flying are usually males. The male fireflies flash in flight to signal a female. As they fly, they look around to see if any females flash back.

The female fireflies usually perch in the grass or on shrubs, watching for the males. When a female sees a flashing male, she might choose to flash back. When a male spots a female flashing with the right pattern, he may decide to fly to her. Then they mate. Soon after mating, the female lays eggs.

There are thousands of different types, or species, of fireflies. Some species flash and others do not. Each kind of flashing firefly has a different flash pattern. So a firefly must carefully watch for the flashing pattern of its own species to find a mate. You can begin to recognize these patterns by counting the seconds between each flash. The firefly species that do not flash use their sense of smell instead of a flashing pattern to find a mate.

A few weeks after the female lays eggs, the eggs hatch into larvae. One interesting thing about fireflies is that they are in the larva stage for about two years! During this time, they live underground and eat earthworms, snails, and other soft-bodied animals. That means fireflies spend most of their lives looking like this:

In late spring, a firefly larva becomes a pupa, and a few weeks later an adult emerges. When they finally become adults, many fireflies don't eat at all! Adult fireflies live for only a few weeks, and in that time, they are on a mission to find a mate. There's not much time for eating!

Fireflies are sometimes called lightning bugs, but they aren't really flies or bugs. They are beetles. Beetles are insects that have two pairs of wings, a sturdy set on top and a delicate pair underneath.

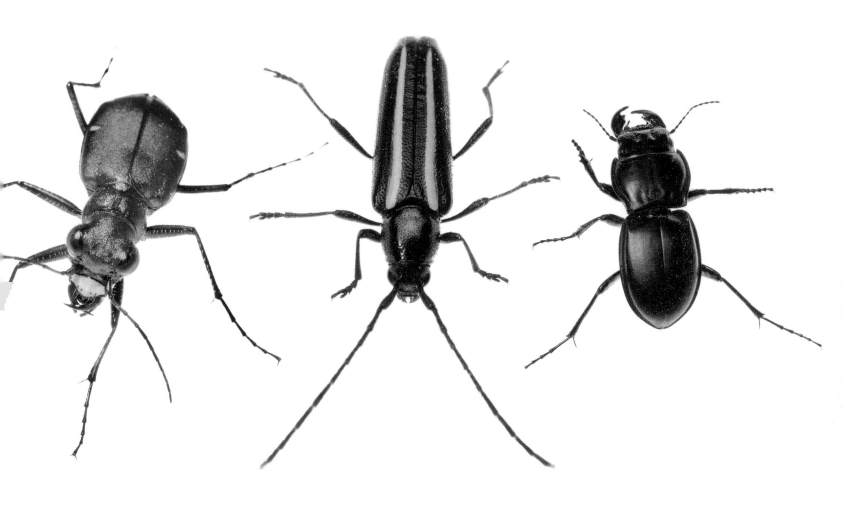

June bugs, ladybugs, and fireflies are all types of beetles. Beetles usually have a straight line down their backs where the outer wings come together. Can you find this line on each of the beetles on these pages?

The top pair of a firefly's wings are not as hard as most beetles' outer wings. They are more leathery. This makes fireflies more fragile than most beetles. So always be gentle when you hold them in your hands.

To fly, fireflies hold out their top wings and flap the wings underneath.

If you want to get a closer look at fireflies, you can catch them and place them in a jar. The safest way is to use a net. Once you catch them in the net, gently push them from the net into the container. Be sure there are airholes at the top, so the fireflies can breathe, and a moist paper towel at the bottom, so the fireflies don't dry out. Observe the fireflies for a short while, then set them free.

When you look closely at a firefly, you will see that like all adult insects, it has six legs.

You will also notice that fireflies have very large eyes to help them see at night.

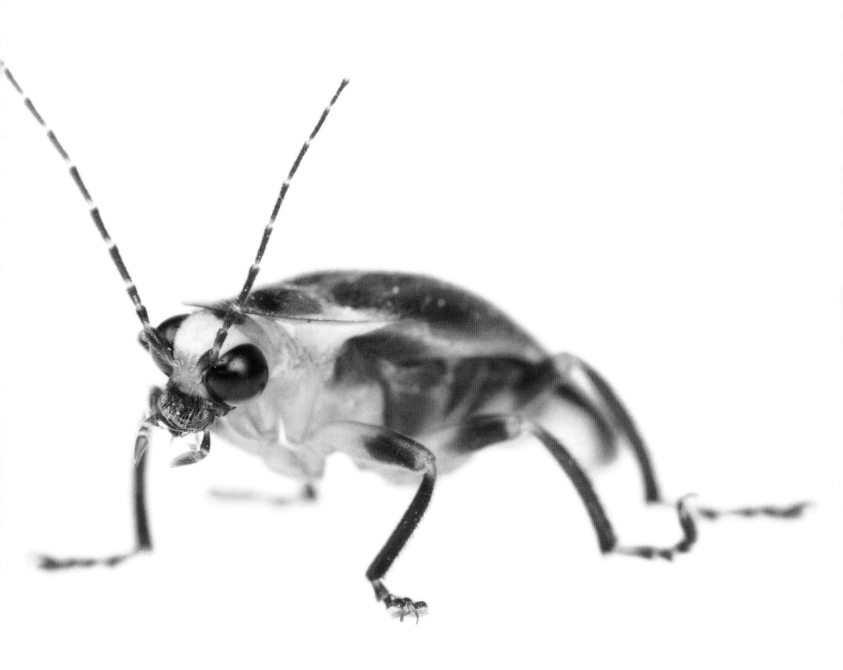

The most fascinating part of the firefly is its lantern, the part that lights up. Chemicals inside the lantern combine with oxygen in the air to produce light.

You may think it is dangerous for fireflies to flash at night because predators can easily find them. It's true that fireflies can be seen by beetle-eating animals such as bats and frogs, but these predators learn to avoid fireflies because they taste terrible! The flashing light actually warns predators *not* to eat the fireflies.

There are a few species of fireflies that will actually flash all together in unison. They are called synchronous fireflies. Scientists aren't sure why these fireflies behave this way, but they think it might be all the males trying to be the first one to signal the females, or that the males have a better chance of being seen by the females if they all flash together. This is quite an extraordinary sight, but the reason remains a mystery.

So the next time you see a firefly, remember that it flashes with its special pattern to find a mate. It was a larva living underground for years—eating, growing, and changing. And finally, this summer, it has its chance to fly ... and flash ... and mate! Isn't that remarkable?

ABOUT THE PHOTOS

Synchronous fireflies,
Great Smoky Mountains National Park
(Judd Patterson)

Holding a firefly
(Steven David Johnson)

Firefly taking flight
(Steven David Johnson)

Observing fireflies
(Steven David Johnson)

Firefly in flight
(Terry Priest)

Firefly perched on a leaf
(Terry Priest)

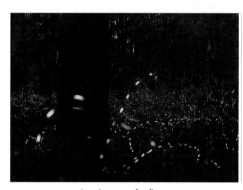

Synchronous fireflies,
Great Smoky Mountains National Park
(Judd Patterson)

Firefly larva
(Clay Bolt)

Adult firefly
(Clay Bolt)

Adult firefly
(Clay Bolt)

Ox beetle (*Strategus aloeus*)
(Seth Patterson)

Ladybug
(Clay Bolt)

Ground beetle
(Clay Bolt)

Six-spotted tiger beetle
(Clay Bolt)

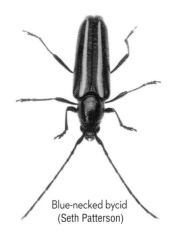

Blue-necked bycid
(Seth Patterson)

Firefly perched on finger
(Steven David Johnson)

Firefly in flight
(Terry Priest)

Firefly in flight
(Terry Priest)

Catching fireflies in a jar
(Steven David Johnson)

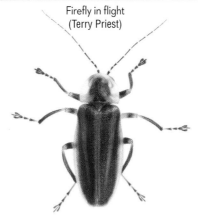

Adult firefly
(Seth Patterson)

Firefly face
(Seth Patterson)

Holding a firefly
(Steven David Johnson)

Flashing fireflies
(Steven David Johnson)

Firefly taking flight
(Steven David Johnson)

Activities to Encourage a Sense of Wonder About Fireflies

❖ Place a firefly in a jar or bug box. Sketch it, and label the following parts: legs, wings, antennae, lantern, and eyes.

❖ Catch another type of beetle in a separate jar or bug box. Compare it to the firefly. What is the same? What is different?

❖ Try to identify the species of fireflies in your area by their flashing patterns. You can download a chart containing the patterns of various fireflies at *www.mos.org/fireflywatch/images/MOS_FFW_Firefly_Flash_Chart.pdf.*

❖ Pretend you are a firefly. Gather some friends and several flashlights. Create flashing patterns by intermittently covering the lighted end of a flashlight with your hand or a piece of paper. Have a friend repeat your pattern with another flashlight.

❖ Become a part of the Boston Museum of Science's Firefly Watch project, where you can make observations of fireflies in your backyard to help scientists with their research. Visit *www.mos.org/fireflywatch.*

❖ Make a list of questions you still have about fireflies. Do some research to find the answers.

Websites

Boston Museum of Science Firefly Watch
www.mos.org/fireflywatch

Firefly Facts, Pictures, and Information
www.firefly.org

Next Time You See
www.nexttimeyousee.com

Downloadable classroom activities with student pages
can be found at *www.nsta.org/nexttime-firefly.*